Connecting Routes

Connecting Routes

poems by

Elayna Mae Darcy

ELIXIRVERSEPRESS.COM

Copyright © 2025 Elayna Mae Darcy

All rights reserved. No part of this publication may be reproduced, distributed, or transmitted in any form or by any means, including photocopying, recording, or other electronic or mechanical methods, without the prior written permission of the publisher, except in the case of brief quotations embodied in critical reviews and certain other noncommercial uses permitted by copyright law.

Book Design by C. Brennecke.
Illustrations by Elayna Mae Darcy

ISBNs: 978-1-7323540-7-4 (Paperback)
        978-1-7323540-8-1 (eBook)
        978-1-7323540-9-8 (Audio Book)

First Edition, July 2025

Magic Key Media in partnership with Elixir Verse Press
elixirversepress.com

DEDICATION

*For the poets
we may never know—
consider this
your call to adventure.*

Table of Contents

DEPARTURES

Nexus 1
Berth 2
The First Commandment 4
You Too 5
Waiting in the Rain 8
Each Moment I'm Given 9
After the Before 10
On Each Other's Shoulders 11
An Ode to the Cloister at the Art Museum 12
Open Air 15
The Bus is Not a Bus 16
Gone to Inspiration 18
An Ode to the Man in Good Karma 19
Outrun 21
What We Hold 22
The Road Chosen 23
Here Was Finished 24
On the Way Home from Home 25
The 43 26
Germantown Clip Show 27
That Night in Atlantis 30

ROUTES

- Through Self, to Sea 35
- Atlantic City in Three Acts 36
- Searchlights 40
- The 23 41
- Secret Artists 42
- Portal Fantasy 43
- Each Verse a Star 45
- Today's Sacred Sinners 46
- This is About a Tree (& a Little About Me) 49
- Even the Embers* 50
- Gender Euphoria 52
- They Are 53
- Fire Hydrant 55
- If You Can 56
- Rise, and Shine 59
- The Villain 62
- Typos on the 2 64
- Depression Feels Like 65
- A Poem About Not Being Able to Write a Poem . 66
- Wondering All at Once 68
- This Present When 69
- SEPTAdelic 70
- Out of the Woods, Yet 71
- The 54 73

I Was There 74

DESTINATIONS

Whirl Away 77
Excerpts from the Last Day of Therapy 78
Identification? Please. 79
Not Anymore 80
Made It Out 81
The Protagonist 82
Forged Friends 83
Plurality 84
Per Aspera 85
Living Names 86
What We Survived 87
Your Turn Now 89
Your Definition 90
Elegy for the Lost Poems 91
Spring Garden, an Entendre 92
Making My Mark 93
Body & Soul 95
How Rich 96
I Am Two 97
El of the Road, a Prologue 98
Illuminate Me 100
A Blessing from the 3 101

Let It	102
I Know Now	103
The True Hero's Journey	105
One Answer	106
The First Commandment, Revisited	108
World Wielder	109
Next Stop	111
ACKNOWLEDGEMENTS	115
ABOUT THE AUTHOR	119

"Departures,"

NORWOOD LANE

BORO LINE RD

Nexus

Some streets in our lives can be sirens,
calling us back to them again and again,
like a piece of us belongs to them.

If there were a nexus to me,
I imagine it would be on the corner of
Germantown Avenue & Broad Street.

I've lived many lives along these lay lines,
yet the more new places to which
I wander, the more of myself I find.

Berth

This road might know me
better than I know myself,
connecting two distant eras
that shaped me into being.

I don't know
what this next chapter holds,
but my soul knows
the turn of time enough now
to recognize that this one
must be captured to tell
the truth of my story.

These plastic blue seats
will take a few hundred years
to decay and biodegrade,
but here we are,
riding them anyway,
though we'll be dust again
long before the earth
erodes them down to the same.

This bus makes us
beings in motion,
traversing spaces
that make sense to us.
We wander through the chaos
passengers of the moment.

"This is my stop," someone nearby says
as they bid goodbye to a friend.
then make their way for the exit.
As they go, my heart whispers,
"You are just beginning..."

The First Commandment

The broken sign demanded,
"PEN! PEN! PEN!"
and who I am not to listen
when the signs are this loud?
When the universe wants me
to write so much it starts
communicating through
Kensington Ave storefronts,
that's how I know what I'm creating
is merely something borrowed,
and the creation is what
I am giving back.

You Too

Next, I had to rebuild,
and admit to the power
I'd always held within,
quietly knowing who I could be.

In that era of collapsing inward,
of navigating memoryscapes,
mindfields, and several ends of days,
I found out there was to be
so much more to my story.

As I readied for
my thirty-fourth revolution,
cosmic shifts helped me to see
that there was nothing left to fear
except staying the same.
The more I let myself unravel,
the more hope found me.

I stopped trying to escape time
and sat with it in a chain coffee shop.

Objects in my headspace
started drifting into place.

I can feel in my bones,
the dust of this nebula is settling,
revealing that like a TARDIS,
my soul has always been
bigger on the inside.
My identity stopped
hiding between the lines,
and started living out loud.
Together,
in the silence,
at my a table carved
by my grandfather's hand,
with nothing separating me
from that voice inside,
at last,
I heard them.
I found them.

And though they still
speak in a whisper,
I know they speak truth.

You are here.
You are light.
You are still
becoming you...

Waiting in the Rain

Fleeting instances,
moments that never strike twice.
The storm is over,
but so is this raindrop of a hello
between two people who
do not know each other,
and who will never
meet eyes or smiles again.

"Don't get caught in the rain!"

"I won't..." I try to promise,
before we go our separate ways.

Each Moment I'm Given

Writing while riding the bus
hits different these days.

After so long in isolation,
every person I encounter
feels like a miracle.

I don't know why any of us survived,
why we're the ones who made it out alive,
and who knows how long any of us have left
before Death comes to collect what is Theirs.

All I know is I'm making the most
of each moment I'm given,
still smiling,
even if no one can see it.

After the Before

We went outside,
felt the air for the first time
in months that felt like years.
We laughed beneath
strings of warm fairy lights
and a canopy of vines,
eating wings and pretzels,
sipping sparkling wine
from disposable plastic cups.

For a moment,
I forget we're in The After now,
because this brief absence of masks
tastes like beer cheese and The Before.

On Each Other's Shoulders
—after Amanda Gorman

She captivated an entire broken nation.
With mere minutes and words
and delicate gestures of her hands,
she began a resuscitation, her breath
filled up our lungs again with hope's oxygen,
as she reminded us our pain deserved validation.

Amanda, standing on Maya's shoulders,
wearing caged birds on her ears,
showed us there is a way forward,
that there are sunlit paths before us,
only if we do not forget all the darkness
of the past that lies behind us.

An Ode to the Cloister at the Art Museum

I'm off to see beauty and exist
alone
amidst artists' ghosts.

Their fingerprints are the reasons we remember.

I go to a place where
I've always felt safe
—the Cloister—
a recreation of an abbey from
some seven hundred years ago.

I wonder about who
worshiped here,
among these pieces of past,
about who rebuilt
the bench on which I sit
so I can feel for a moment
I am not where I am.
The fountain babbles.
The children flow.
Generational whispers echo.

I do not come here
for the religiosity,
but instead for
something real—
a spiritual connection
that exists only in art,
in our representations
of the everyday divinity
that so often goes unnoticed.

Families amble
through the exhibit
as I sit alone and smile,
wondering what the monks
might think of who we
as a people have become.

My hope,
is that even across
the ages and the changes,
that they would see

we still create,
and that they'd know
our very existence
is the most powerful
kind of prayer.

Open Air

I forgot how fresh laughter sounds
when it drifts through open air,
mixing with music that's always
about how we only have tonight.

I stopped believing
the sun's rise is promised,
and don't know how long it will be
before we can look in each other's eyes again
and see the truth of them
without whom they are so obscured.

I wish I could bottle this crisp,
carefree air to use as a cleanser
when I'm back to being
locked in my house for
who knows how much longer.

What I wouldn't give to bathe
in this evening's breeze when
life becomes too much again.

The Bus is Not a Bus

Greater minds than mine
have long since realized that
the pipe is not a pipe.
An image of a thing
is not itself, the thing.

Yet my unskilled sketch
of this parked bus in front of me
could not be more the thing.

I believe every rendering
shares part of the soul
of the one who created it.

My meager verses and doodles
have in their existing
captured something untouchable,
yet achingly tangible.

With ink and thought,
I made this personal close up
of a parked bus, in a way, immortal.

Every stroke of hope adds
another stanza to the story.

Gone to Inspiration

The muses are off to rest,
to replenish their wells
and soak in rays of new ideas
they might inspire.

Meanwhile, I'm still here,
trying to fend off the fear
that I've forgotten how to create.

As I await their return,
I learn to harness my own magic,
see what moments
I might inspire.

An Ode to the Man in Good Karma

Good sir, you feel like a mirror to my future.
Sitting there with your several sweaters
and relentless scrawl across the pages
of your clearly well loved notebook.

I wonder what world your mind is in.
Are you here? Grounded in
facts and equations,
with vital business to attend to?
Or does your mind wander
to worlds undiscovered?
Are you mapping the through lines
to self, or spitting out the lyrics
to some song that was almost
lost like a chime on the wind?

All this stuff around us is life,
this coffee, these tables,
these cells shaped by
a few hundred million years
of forged and wrought stardust.

In you I see that my life
can be built on a
foundation of stories.
I see that I,
and you, and all this
existential drudgery is
itself what matters most.

That we are the question.
That we are that we ask.
That we are the wonder that wanders.

Outrun

Today the words don't come easy.
I search my insides for meanings
that I haven't penned yet,
for the songs I've held in unsung.
I ask my heart for the truths of me,
to put to verse the things
I cannot outrun.

What We Hold

Transpasses and prayer beads.
Sacred objects that we fiddle with
between fingers and run thumbs over.
Things we hold onto
that get us from
one place to the next.
Out of both grow
prayers and poems,
plastic manifestations
of faith in something
within and beyond ourselves.
Brick and stone shrines
can only do so much
when the largest parts of life
are lived here on the road
and in the in-between.

The Road Chosen
—after Robert Frost

I got lost on the way to myself,
forced down wrong turns
and back alleys of trauma,
rerouted relentlessly until
I've entirely forgotten
the name of the road
I started from.

I come to a crossroads
at the corners of Insanity Row
and Do Things Different Lane,
where the fog is so thick I can't tell
where either route will lead.

So I look to the words of poets past,
and ask of my heart
to guide me down the desire path
of Do Things Different Lane,
in hopes that one day,
it will make all the difference.

Here Was Finished

There's a pattern in my life
of endings,
and facing them
alone...
no one by my side
at the eleventh hour's goodbye.

Gone will be all the trappings
of the life lived within those walls,
everywhere empty of the objects
and the memories that happened there.
Nothing but the musty air,
and a promise that
I'm leaving because
here was finished,
and there is ready,
waiting for me...

On the Way Home from Home

My hometown moved on without me.
New legends and distilleries
that have nothing to do with
the family that raised me.
Firehouses and bars that don't remember
my grandfather's loving legacy.

It's strange to see a place that shaped you,
and realize it never needed you in order to continue.

It was always going to exist
with or without you.

The 43

November air bites,
This damn bus is late again.
Runs on borrowed time.

Germantown Clip Show

I write this as I pass hundreds of graves
along a road that's rich with personal lore.
The colors still burst along the avenue,
but the memories from when
I lived this way feel like they're
lost in a tragic grayscale.

I imagine a sepia tinted past
where I saw you
for who you were sooner.

My body keeps the score
the closer we get to that place
where the power went out
the night before the apocalypse.
But you seized that momentary
darkness and lit every gas lamp,
before spending two years
convincing me of realities
that turned out to be
lying shadow puppets.

There were good memories too,
defenestrating Christmas trees
and YouTube marathons on the projector,
but I'll never drink from
a Barefoot bottle again
as long as I live because of you.

You were the one who
concretized my fear that
the people I love will leave me.

You ruined so much more than you built,
you pushed away every hand
that reached to pull you out
of lies you've been telling yourself.

For all the horrors,
I do miss the rare joys.
But I refuse to spend another
minute of my life waiting

for a friend that I gave my all to,
to realize that his puzzles
won't mourn him when he's gone.

Not like I would.

Not like I did.

That Night in Atlantis

How could I have known
that night in Atlantis
would be the one that
disappeared a decade
of friendship into the ocean?

I've tried to remember
what we both said,
but all I have left of it
are angry, scribbled hieroglyphs
of an argument that
drowned you out of my life.

The aftermath was
months of feeling lost at sea.
I was splintered driftwood
that believed it was my own fault
I'd been thrown into the water,
like your arm wasn't the one
that cast me out for refusing
to be who you wanted me to be.

I thought life without you
would be the end of me,
that you'd be the last one I'd lose,
before finally deciding
to surrender to the tides,
and let Poseidon punish me
for always hoping too much.

It turned out that hope
was what kept me afloat
until I washed up on new shores,
and realized there were
entire worlds of joy
and freedom beyond
the lost island of You.

Routes

BROAD ST.

GERMANTOWN AVE.

Through Self, to Sea

Day dreaming my morning away.
Romanticizing every facet of my life
as I waltz through the day in a haze of hope.
It's as if I've finally unlocked
and walked through a door to myself
that I never believed would budge.
I thought it jammed shut,
sealed tight like a tomb.
But now that I've made
my way through, I've discovered
an entirely new
dimension of identity.
As a human, kindness
is our nature,
we hold so many
fathoms of being,
our wells of self
run planet deep.
What metaphors we are.

Atlantic City in Three Acts

I.
Every trip we ever took to the shore,
I'd keep the windows down
so I would be able to smell
the ocean once we were close enough.
I'd shiver with excitement,
earnest for that first whiff of salt water,
the taste of butterscotch and chocolate fudge,
and getting to people watch
with my mom on the boardwalk.

II.
Today I find myself on a pilgrimage to the past.
I'm going to my mother's favorite place,
and in a way, where our family began.
There could be nowhere
more sacred to me than this town
that's renowned for its sins.

I stood at the edge,
close enough to see

but not enough to touch.
This is my life's divine metaphor
that I am tired of being true.
If this next chapter of my life
holds nothing else,
let it grab fistfuls of joy
where every grain of sand
is just another memory.

III.
"I'm going to catch the sunrise,"
I said to the NJ transit guy
when he asked, confused,
what I was doing on the
2am bus from Philly to AC.

Getting there was otherworldly.
You haven't seen strange until
you've seen the Atlantic City Boardwalk
emptied of every single person.

I find a rock by the water
from which to witness our rising star
as it climbs into the sky
behind Steel Pier's ferris wheel.

On my feet and with
a leg still wounded,
I risk the water because
a week from now,
I'll get to stand in the Pacific,
and there's a poetry
to standing in both oceans
in such short order.

I summon the Atlantic
like I am shouting to a friend,
and the gentle waves
come up to bless my toes.
As the ancient water
reaches my skin,
I know that within me,
healing is happening at last.

But damn,
do I wish my mom
was here with me to feel it...

Searchlights

Searchlights slice
      through the foggy night
and I wonder what
      they're looking for.
Like me, they seem
      to wander aimlessly
not knowing their
      target, uncertain...
unsure... but still
      they have a purpose,
something to find,
      and whether that's
distant planets or
      just peace of mind,
they keep looking
      upward and onward
paths crossing and then not,
      like remembering a destiny
they somehow forgot.

The 23

The only refuge.
Lost world between house and work,
where I found the words.

Secret Artists

You exist
everywhere around me.
Drawing as I'm writing.
Humming as I'm thrumming
with the creative magic
that exists deep within us all.

Some listen closely,
waiting for inspiration
to whisper softly,
while others drown it out,
loudly touting distractions
that take them further
away from themselves.

I'd like to believe that if
creativity were a person,
they wouldn't force us to make,
but they would implore us all to listen.

Portal Fantasy

Sitting beside a portal to Lithuania
before catching the 32.

In being here, the most interesting thing
is not the portal itself, as much as it is
the human fascination that walks by it.
The hopeful ingenuity that built it.

The excitement of an elderly gentleman
who walked past so he could wave
to the strangers in Poland,
even as his son grumbled to his mother,
"can we please just keep moving?"

A small chorus of children
wish a Merry Christmas
to people on the other side of the world.
The group of teens, who giggling incessantly,
gave the atmosphere the bird before running off.

How we delight at the strange.

How we all starve for connection.

The people who pass by
without a glance are somehow
louder than the ones calling out hello.
The ones who stand silent and stare–
I wonder what their inner soliloquy sounds like.

I wonder if they all feel
this connectedness humming
through their being the same
way that I always have,
even when it was something
I didn't know how to name.

Each Verse a Star
—*after Nikita Gill's 93% Stardust*

Once you showed me
I was made of stardust,
the poetry poured out of me.

Words began pooling into galaxies,
each verse a star in the constellation of my story.

Your poems helped me unravel
the passion I'd been hiding within me
like a solar flare trapped in a bottle.

Through your words,
I learned to reach deep
into the depths of my darkness,
and it was there that I
sharpened my strength
as a whetstone does a sword.

Your kindness forged a storm in me,
and all life has been a poem since.

Today's Sacred Sinners

In the Pantheon of Poetry, you'll find many patron saints and deities. Some of these heroes are long gone, while others still roam the crossroads of our late capitalist Americana. Some of their names you know, and some of them, you don't.

There's Jack Keroauc, Patron Saint of Lost Roads and Wanderers.

Mary Oliver, Guardian Angel of Nature's Stillness and Quiet Contemplations.

Nikita Gill, Demi-Goddess of All that is Wild and Wonder.

Amanda Lovelace, Our Lady of Mad Books and Bewitching Hopes.

Maya Angelou, Mother of Unapologetic Self Love.

Then there is Ari Koontz, a star-named poet whose multitudes include intergalactic druid and woodland venturer. Dirt beneath their fingernails, they sift the soil in search of seeds that they will nurture into stories. Their every word, a nourishing morsel prepared with careful hands.

There is C. Brennecke, perhaps not first of her name, but nevertheless a breaker of chains. A modern priestess of actualization through art, a reincarnated Oracle of Philadelphia, and diviner of elixired verses.

There's Jay Atlas, a man whose name tells you where he's been—crisscross walked a nation, following the veins and meridian lines of these Divided States, while he bears the rest of a world he's never seen on his high-school-football-injured shoulders.

Then there's people like me, the as-yet nobodies who write of anonymous Aphrodites they've met in the darkened corners of dive bars. Queers who've hopped into the bumper cars of Tattooed Moms, only to be ferried off for cheese fries and shots of whiskey with Persephone.

But the thing about us nobodies that nobody realizes, is we are the verses that come next.

We are what the future has in store—the ones we hope next generations will remember well, even if we didn't take enough care of ourselves while we were here to live the stories.

This is About a Tree (& a Little About Me)

They cut her down.
I watched as they sawed away
at her piece by piece,
that peaceful creature who spent
decades growing & overcoming
everything the elements rained down on her.

They tore her limb from limb
though she did nothing to warrant it.

They deemed her branches & body
as too unruly to be allowed to continue.

There's nothing left now but a stump
and the inner rings that tell of things
she survived—evidence of a life
that the world hacked apart.

*Even the Embers**

In that beautiful season
we were both tried by fire
in the softest of ways.

We were not thrown,
howling into a blaze
that would seek to teach us
that the only road to success
must be one paved in suffering.

Together we learned
we could be marshmallows,
gently toasting and cozy
while we lose ourselves to
the campfire songs
and longing tales
that others had to spin.

We reached within,
where we found that
kindness can be fiery too—
warm and inviting,

teaching us by the light
to love & find beauty
even in the embers.

previously published in Elixir Verse Equinox: Terra Verses

Gender Euphoria

There's days when I'm a bright star burning,
when my confidence could take on
the universe and come out of it victorious.

Those days of gender euphoria
might be few and far between,
but they remind me that I
hold the power of both King & Queen,
that I am sovereign of my own body,
and no one gets to tell me how to live in it.

They Are
—after Jan Phillips' "He Is, She Is"

From the One, the New is born.
They are the aroma of dust after rain,
and they are the clouds, golden rosé
after the storm passes and the thunder quiets.

They are fireflies in the summer night trees,
bright blinks amidst darkness, illuminations
that warm the quiet and cricket-song.

They are the light in your eyes when
you've opened up to understand
something you once thought impossible.

They are the mist from the waves
that caresses your face
when you close your eyes
and stand small against the sprawling sea.

They are the iridescence that catches
on the wall when a beam kisses a prism,
and the whole spectrum kisses back.

They are the sparkle in stone surfaces,
in your eyelashes, and in the heavens.
They are all that is man and magic.
They are all that is woman and wonder.
They are infinitely beyond and
foundationally within.
They are breathing.
They are being.
They are beginning.

Fire Hydrant

They matched the fire hydrants,
a brilliant blood-orange splattered
over the late September grey.
They were the sun on a clouded street,
overlooked by a loving guardian rainbow.

Though the paint on the street
fades with weather and time,
the blood stains don't.
We remember the Queens
and their heels on the necks
of those who would rather erase us.

As we walk roads paved with
that pain and that pride,
we will immortalize
our lost and our stolen,
doing everything we can
to remind those who follow after us
that we won't let them
suffer this world alone
in the ways that we were made to.

If You Can

Softly, she said,
"These last few weeks have been traumatic..."
and the conversation held within it
a moment of reverent silence.

What more is there to say
when innocents are slaughtered,
funded by a state that steals land
and spins false narratives into being?

In a country running out of coins—
where mothers can't feed their babies,
but the billionaires built on blood diamonds
can buy platforms of protest
to silence a resistance into sadness—
I still exist.

Detergent prices double while the dryer is broken,
and the fridge needs fixing, and somehow
our bandwidth is supposed to withstand this.

The world outside the bus
crumbles around us,
but she softly asks,
"Are you an artist?"

Her words send me to another dimension,
where I imagine myself in a cottage by the sea,
trading my line of sky for one of shore.
I'm an artist there the most;
in my imagination where not a single limit exists.
In my art and my stories, I can do anything.

When she softly asks, "What's your medium?"
I stutter my way through an answer.

I should have said hope and ink,
the two things that make me
feel like a star-forged being,
powerful and infinite.

The silence that follows sits peacefully between us.

These are the most genuine words
I've exchanged with a stranger in
I-don't-even-know-how-long a time.
But it makes me scramble
for my journal and a pen.

I may never see this woman again.

Even when the world is free-falling,
I'm holding on, telling tales of rising.

As I gather my bags to leave
this moment and this bus behind,
there are six last words she softly says.

"Get some rest, if you can."

Rise, and Shine

The day is November 6th, 2024,
and the sun had the audacity to rise.
Never before have I been so offended by her light.
Doesn't she know that we stopped deserving her a long time ago?
Her photons are not strong enough to pierce
hardened, hating hearts.
Doesn't she know that when she set yesterday,
she took a hope-filled future with her?

I have always been slow to anger,
but on this particular morning,
I punched a traffic pole on 11th Street,
as I called out a homophobe
right to his face.
I'd overheard him mumble
to the traveler beside him,
"He's gonna keep these gays out of the White House.
Never should have let 'em there in the first place."

I called him an asshole,
and while it wasn't my finest moment
it was something I needed to release.

I'm so tired of being quiet
while white supremacy
makes a day job of genocides.

The world doesn't get better
by relying on hope alone.
The time for calling out
hatred to its face is always.

Everyone, everywhere,
who holds a modicum of privilege
needs to suck it up,
and make a fucking ruckus
so that trans kids, Palestinians,
Black Americans, South Asians,
and every other person
white nationalists seek to erase
gets to live safe, joyous, and free.

From the river to the sea,
from small town Texas to a poisoned DC,
for the love of love,
let's punch some fascists in the teeth.

The Villain

I guess 32's as good a time as any
to enter my "villain" era.

My close friends would agree
these boundaries set
to protect me are overdue—
that I should have started
defending myself more
a long time ago.

Meanwhile, the ones who
kept me trapt in survival mode,
second guessing my very existence,
have moved on,
busy painting me
in unflattering shadows.

Some people are not happy
unless they are a victim,
even when the hurt
is something wrought
with their own hands.

You only get abused so many times
before you realize that
you never needed permission
to protect your own peace.

So if standing up for who I want to be
makes me your enemy?
Then call me the Darkling,
darling, and "go ahead,
make me your villain."

Typos on the 2

"on her phone without friendships"
except the text was supposed to say
"on her phone without headphones"
but my brain made an Elaynian slip
and now I can't stop thinking
about the implications of
"on her phone without friendships"
because what must it say about me
that my mind made that up?
that in the moments where I stop thinking,
I'm ever wondering of what a dismal life
this would be without the people who love me?

Depression Feels Like

I lay on my back looking up at the sky,
knowing it is filled with stars and stories.
Yet here in the city, I can scarcely see any,
and so despite their presence,
I feel uneasy and alone.

Staring skyward,
knowing that the hope is there,
shining and begging you to see it,
but life has blocked it out,
rendered the sky a void,
leaving you to wonder
if you'll ever see the light again.

A Poem About Not Being Able to Write a Poem

Sometimes I pull out my pen
and my mind goes entirely
b l a n k

These moments, I feel as a failure.
A magician who has suddenly dropped all their cards.
A teacher who has no lessons left to give.
A puppeteer whose dolls have all cut their strings
to run off and become real children without them.

In these times of divine un-inspiration,
my blood runs cold with fear.
Do I have anything left to say?
Thankfully, the answer's always the same.

Of-fucking-course I do.

Eventually, the emptiness of the page
begs enough that I scrounge up metaphors
like loose change in the forgotten
pockets of my bookbag.

I find verses like they are
keys dropped on the street.
I discover new ways for the words
to make a meaning, like rerouting
a GPS when one's gotten lost.

That may be why words have been the love of my life.
They exist always as familiar and new,
as friend and stranger, as forever and now,
as finite expressions of
i n f i n i t y

Wondering All at Once
—after all the songs that saved me

There are certain verses you just keep coming back to,
no matter how far away you've dared to move.
These faded p!nk and fraying songs that
dripped with aching enchantment,
became the anthems that
sang me into survival during
a timeless age
of young and hopeless teenage pain
where every hurt felt like
it would last all of my days.

In the end, I know there will never be
a way for me to thank every artist
whose lyrics raised me up,
but without them,
the rest of my story would
have remained forever unwritten.

This Present When

Lately the days drip with
all the apathy of a leaking sink.
I feel like time stopped meaning
what it once did, ever since I had to
distance myself from it
and from everyone else.

Now, I'm just here.
Not later.
Not then.
Just waltzing through
this present when,
where I'm awakening
to all these illusions I
used to believe were reality.

As motorcycles roar by and the clock tower chimes,
I find myself more here than
any of the theres I've ever been.
I'm swimming in this wine and this divine air
that fills the end of the most lonesome summer,
hoping and waiting for an autumn wind of change.

SEPTAdelic

Turns out the pillars of swallowing smoke
were just long reflections of ceiling lights—
an illusion to an eye trained
to see the art in everything.

Don't be afraid to be
a soul who seeks the beauty
where no one expects it to be.

Out of the Woods, Yet
—after Taylor Swift

Eyes closed,
I am wandering through the woodland.
Acoustic heart with love on a string,
whimsical leaves and lover's arms.
Sprawling branches reach for
the light between piano keys.

Eyes open,
I'm a metal gear,
here, seated, stuck.
Tired, balding wheels
shape stranger's sadness.
I'm caught in dusty air vents
of an old, ink-black chevy.

Eyes closed again,
I'm tossing pennies in the pool,
dying, but not staying dead,
and learning to live long instead.

I morph through and to these poetic unrealities
that only exist in the midnight dark.

In this soundscape, I am my
innermost dreamings personified.

In these verses, I can be out of the woods
into who I've always wanted to be,
this mess of a dreamer
with the nerve to adore myself.

The 54

Growth of a lifetime,
along the length of Lehigh.
Whole worlds discovered.

I Was There

This park has a beating heart,
one made of SEPTA sounds
& birdsong & whispering trees
& water dancing &
people coming & going.

Here holds a mystic magnetism
of creative energy that begs
the artist in me to create.
I'm meant to soak in a city, to wash away
the pain of living, to give birth
to the joy of existing.

My story is one of many
that has wandered through
the metal gates into this
metropolitan magic garden,
but it's one I must put to paper
to remember I was here.

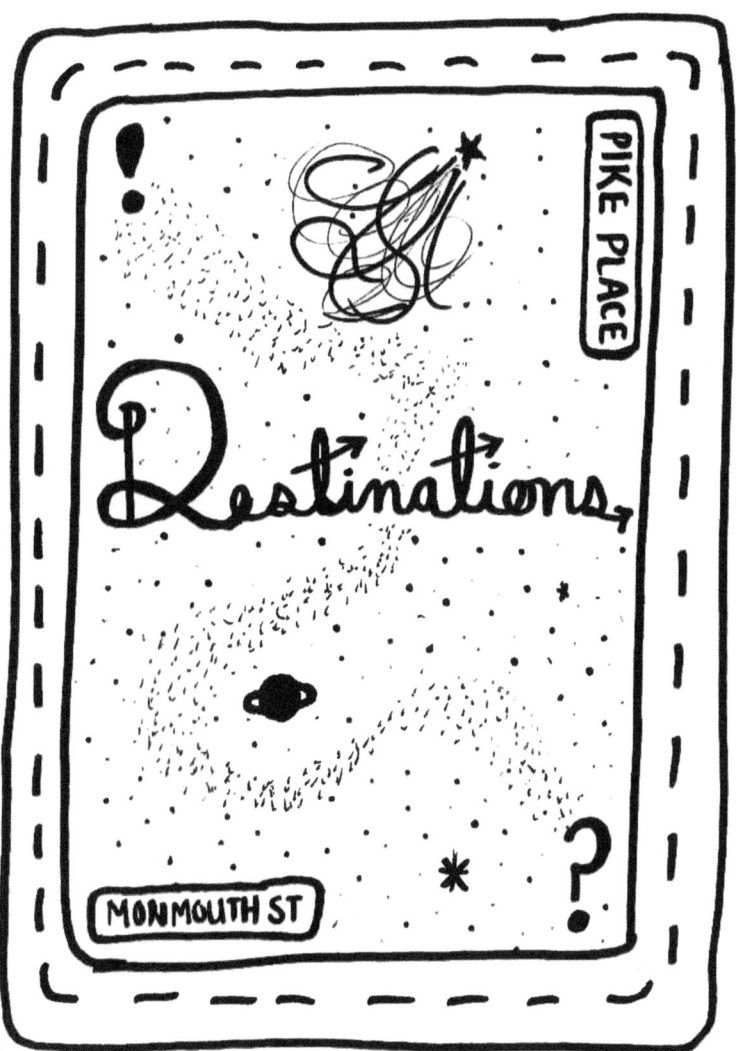

Whirl Away

I was a dandelion seed
crushed into the spine
of a long forgotten story,
forged in the quiet dark.

But crack open the tome
and watch me whirl away,
dancing forth to plant myself
in a soul that deserves me.

Excerpts from the Last Day of Therapy

THEM
"I'm so beyond proud of you."

"It's beautiful how you are and who you are."

"You're such a light, and I knew it in the first two minutes of my first day."

"Your joy is infectious, maddeningly so. It's been amazing to know you."

"I'm glad I got to see you decide to stay."

ME
"No matter what, I'll be okay."

Identification? Please.

Why do IDs always make me wax poetic?
Maybe it is the fact that a piece of plastic
is supposed to tell people who I am,
even though to quantify that
would be impossible.

Or perhaps it is that it has an expiration date?
As if I as a person might rot away in the back of a fridge
and need to be replaced by fresh fruit?

Sure, every person dies, but to say I expire
every couple of years and must reaffirm
my existence to a government that otherwise
doesn't give a shit just starts to feel silly.
How strange we humans are
that we think we can explain who it is
we are on a wallet sized card.

Not Anymore

Riding by the library and memories of lost summers.
Passing by wonders and places that once
tasted of possibility and street vendor cocoa.

I saw you through the window once,
texted to check it had been you
I saw walking through the park.

I can't do that anymore, even if I were to see you.
You've made it quite clear that my
one major fuck up doesn't deserve forgiveness,
even as those around you are continually
given free license to abuse you.

While I will always hold hope that one day
you may forgive me and again call me friend,
I refuse to waste my days in lament
when instead I could be living.

Made It Out

I had to come back to the beginning
to understand just how far I've come.
Soon I'll be reset from
the someone who lived here,
that lost shadow self who will
somehow always be a part of me.

I had to revisit the wound,
relive the same solstice in a lonely room,
in order to come out the other side
seeing the strength I've learned
and the resilience I've earned.

I had to come back to the beginning
to understand the beauty of right now.
Because without the journey down
that shadowed path, I'd have never made it out.

The Protagonist

"That's such a main character trait,"
they said, and for just a moment,
in a rare instance of confidence,
I decided to put away the
dishonest demons within and just owned it.
So even though I didn't say it aloud,
I allowed myself to believe it,
"Yeah, maybe it is..."

Forged Friends

Magic manifested
on a
fire escape,
where the
air tasted
of spring
and of
malt liquor.

Two people
who barely
knew each
other opened
their hearts
only to
find there
souls who
knew what
it was
to hide
who you
always were.

Plurality

I wish I'd known sooner
that I could be more than just 'girl'.
That I could be fluid and fire,
a non-binary star, a story
with more stanzas than
pages have room for.
That there being more to me
than I could make sense of
didn't make me wrong.

Per Aspera

If the person you love makes you
contort yourself into a straight,
specific something, when your truth
is that you are beautiful, boundless chaos,
maybe they're the one you want,
but not the one you need.

We were not made in the image
of the universe just to shrink wrap
ourselves into someone else's expectations.

You were made to see through hardship, to the stars.
You were made to love, and feel loved.
You were made to be who you are.

Living Names

We chose our own names
because we knew the ones
they gave us weren't quite right.
Those names now belong
to the children we were,
to the ideas others had of us,
relegated to reliquaries
so we might be reborn
in our own image.

There's no erasing who we've been.
But in each moment we draw breath,
we get to paint the blessing
of who we are into this world,
and that person within us
that we choose to set free
will always be more alive than
anyone's hatred could
ever hope to be.

What We Survived

All that I do anymore
is live, and remember.
I experience the ephemeral,
dwell in each moment like it's my last.
And then, when I can,
I let my pen recollect.
I use my ink to tell
children I'll never meet
that this is what it was like.
This is what we survived.

An endless barrage
of death, and hate, and harm,
pinging to existence in our pockets
while someone making
three times as much as us
expects us to send our little emails.
Twice, we endured
a comic-villain president
who never loved *anyone*,
least of all himself.

On late buses to work
and therapy couches
and laying down at night,
staring at the ceiling wondering
if there will be a tomorrow to wake up to,
we kept going so that some day down the road,
a queer child of color may get to be gifted
the beauty of living in a better
present that we fought to give.

Your Turn Now

I see you in the covers of the books you hold.
These pages where you finally see yourself.
Authors who penned celebrations of identity
that promised you can love who you love
and will still be loved in return.

Barely passed 30 and already I'm a queer elder,
because too many of us have been
hated out of existence before
we could ever grow up.
How I hope the words in that book
and the ones that come after
will save you the way so many of
our lost siblings never got to be.

I hope even one queer child out there
sees these words and knows if
by no one else, they are loved by me.

Your Definition

Pick up a dictionary,
look up your name and see.
There'll be no definition there,
only you write who you'll be.

Elegy for the Lost Poems

I mourn for the earnest verses that died yearning,
never to be etched, lost and wandering
on some lonely mind's highway,
because the writer believed
no one wanted to hear them.

Let this elegy be your call to arms,
your kind reminder that every
hope you've ever had has mattered,
and the universe is begging for
the verses only *you* can pen.

Spring Garden, an Entendre

He was carrying groceries—
a loaf of bread peering over
the edge of the brown paper bag.
He looked up, where a magnolia tree
had burst into bloom in the middle
of Spring Garden Street.
He smiled, a soft reflection
of a world coming back to life.

Making My Mark

Today I sat on the steps of a landmark,
endeavoring to leave my own mark on the land.
All this pavement has been my witness.
Broad Street knows all my secrets.

The clock on the spire has
ticked through my every moment,
seen my flashes of wonder,
my hopeless wandering at her feet,
my many attempts to capture her every angle.
That face has told the time of my survival.
She kept going even after the world stopped
and every stone concourse stood silent,
even if only for a time.

Always, only for a time.

This shuttered school,
this place that gave birth
to so many eras of artists
feels eerie in its ending.

Yet here I am.
Penciling my verse
to this city's artistic legacy,
even if no one ever remembers me.

Body & Soul

One of these things is not like the other.
One is bound in matter, corporeal, tangible, breakable.
The other, ancient, forever, and absolutely unstoppable.
Our bodies serve us with finite purpose
while the spirit serves the maker of the universe.
We were never meant to not believe in ourselves.
We were born as fragments of art, crafted by
the hands of an unendingly loving Artist,
who believed we deserved to be painted.
Every stroke of us matters
to the masterpiece They made us to be.
Our bodies are just vessels for our stories,
the bookbinding to our epic journeys.
Our souls are forged from atoms of wonder,
each moment that we survive, just another word of us.
Who we are was never meant to be defined
by our relationships, our salaries, our degrees.
Who we are is the love we've lived,
the friends we've held, and the hope we've sowed
to be grown long after we're gone.

How Rich

If I looked at every instance lived
as a single coin or precious gem,
oh, how rich am I?

Each second spent
is a memory gained.
Each promise saved,
an understanding earned.

I Am Two

Sitting on the bus,
scrolling through the last 12 months.
The thought that came to mind was
"what a year I've had..."
and the moment I thought it,
it was as if a voice from somewhere deeper,
somehow more me, provided a counterpoint,
"what a life you have..."
My hand flew to my chest
as a soft love overwhelmed my soul.

I've spent too many hours losing myself
to a life I'll never get back,
that I forgot I am alive now,
and I am not some angel
watching over my past self
as if they've died.

I am here now.
I am alive.
I am.
Still...

El of the Road, a Prologue

It's January here in Philly,
and the skyline wears a skin
of even-tempered ocean grey.
All the little huts that make up
the Christmas village have been
stored away until next year.
The seasons are in transition.

By then, I'll be along the west coast
for the final weeks of a most grand adventure.
As I catch my reflection in the Comcast Center's glass,
I wonder if I'll recognize the person
I'll be at the end of the road.

In truth, my hope is that I don't.

I hope for them laugh lines gained along the latitudes,
and that there may be streaks of
this morning's skyline-silver in their hair.

I hope they've helped kids
in the middle of nowhere
realize they deserve
to exist everywhere.

I hope there are more new stories
stacked atop the ones they've already told.
I am already grateful for
all the loved ones they are going to hold.

I know everything will change after the road,
and for once I find myself unafraid,
to run wild into the great unknown.

Illuminate Me

Wandering neon lights follow me
down the concrete paved lane
to destinations planned
but with outcomes untold.

You'd think after all these years I've grown
that maybe so much of my life
wouldn't be this uncertain—
that things would make sense
and that my life's lore would
be already written and scored.

The truth is I have
no idea where I'm going.

Still I keep walking this path ever growing,
as these neon lights illuminate me knowing,
"this is who you are supposed to be."

A Blessing from the 3

A blessing for every person
in the presence of this paper,
every passenger & passerby
& page turner who crosses
paths with this poem.
May you know the deep peace
I feel on this bus on this
misty Monday morning.

Let It

When the hand of someone you love is offered to you, trust it—reach back.

When the sun warms your face, embrace it—soak it in.

When that sense of childlike wonder makes you smile, let it—accept its magic.

When your heart feels ready to let go of old wounds, allow it—move forward with your scars.

They are beautiful, and so too, you are.

I Know Now
—after Mary Oliver's Wild Geese

"You do not have to be good..."
But I used to believe I had to be great.
Anything less than
Charles's Expectations was not enough.
I was doomed to spend my life in an
unending race with myself—
to every minute be better
than who I was before.

I had to be perfect.
Anything shy was abject failure.

"You do not have to be good..."
How I wish I had learned this lesson younger.
I may have taken a scenic route to learn it,
but my gratitude is boundless now
that I'm learning it the long, hard way.
My survival is a testament to the resilience I've gained.

"You do not have to be good..."
Turns out, all I needed was to be.
It is always good to do more good.
To do kind things.
To give love as freely as trees give air.
But through it all, all we must be is who we are.

"You do not have to be good."
How grateful I am to know this now.

I hope one day, you know it too.

The True Hero's Journey

As a kid, I dreamed of
doing something dramatic,
something epic & heroic with my life.
As I near middle age,
I see that maybe the bravest thing
I could ever do would be
to move through the world
letting myself *feel it all*—
the bad, the good, and the beautiful,
the small, the seismic, the stratospheric,
the heartbreaks, the maybes, and the *I love yous*,
the build ups, the break downs, the between spaces.
If I can do more than just survive,
if I can *live* this way,
then I can safely say
at my eventual journey's end,
I saved the one life I could.

One Answer

Why are we here?
What is the sense in any of this?
Or is there not supposed to be?
Sense, that is.
How can it all be chaos when
there is so much deliberate magic
in our everyday lives?

There can be only one answer.

We must be written.

How else does one explain the miraculous?
How can one account for the veins
in our arms being the same
as veins of light in a galaxy?
How does one come to understand
the intricacies of selves and of stories?
How do we manage language
or navigate hope and loss?

There can be only one answer.

We must be written.

The First Commandment, Revisited

"PEN! PEN! PEN!"
the broken sign said again
somewhere around a year later.

O, the things we forgot to repair.
O, the things we get used to.
O, the missing links.
O, the lights snuffed out too soon.

Something about that sign
sounds out a call
to adventure,
by page,
and adventure,
in life.

Who would I be to ignore
my purpose that I have
always known in my bones?

Words are the work,
and the work is the way.

World Wielder

Standing on the first city block I can remember,
about to board a train I've never taken
to a place I've never been.

This misty Tuesday evening, I'm going where I'm loved.

Memories fog the glass of this Quiet Car window,
as city bows to woodland. We barrel through
the town where I was born, but never lived,
heading heart-long into the oblivion
of whatever time I have left.

My next chapter waits unwritten,
an open road where the only place to go is onward.
I'm chasing a life I can't quite articulate
but which I know already exists.

As I kick the dust off
my still holey shoes,
faith paves a path forward.

I've found a family that's scattered
to Earth's four corners,
so no matter where I stand, my ever spinning compass
somehow always manages to point home.

While the players prepare for their places in Act II,
I'm poring back over the manuscript of the first,
wondering if any of it was really enough?
I'm still nothing but a lost bard at Stratford Station,
a beautiful no one, who wields worlds with a word.

So much of my poetry once began
with a plea, *"let me..."*
But standing here and now,
on the first city block I can remember,
I'm no longer begging the universe to let me live in it.

I'm done asking for permission.
I am another chapter, beginning.

Next Stop

Next stop? Inspiration.
Connecting routes to dreams coming true.
(Some) doors are closing
(but others are opening).
Welcome to Route You,
where you'll become who
you're supposed to.
Service to
where you
always belonged.
Thank you for riding
this life.
Next stop…

ACKNOWLEDGEMENTS

To Jay & Noah—as I write these acknowledgements, we are just a few short months from setting out on the journey of a lifetime. While the pages in this book are laced with love for Philly, I am about to see the whole rest of a country with the two of you. I'd be lying to say I'm not a little bit scared to be trading in narrow city streets for wide open highways, but know that there are no humans on this planet that I'd rather have this journey with, and that I'm so grateful for the adventures we've already had, and for all the tales we'll come to tell.

To Christine & Ari & August—you are the friends who exist in my life because stories brought us together. Each of you has managed to come into my life at a moment of time where major shifts were happening in my world, and in your own ways, each of you helped propel me forward into a next level of confidence & craft that make my inner child so proud of who I've become. You are beacons who have helped me heal my shadows, and who have shown me how to harness the light I always had inside of me that I never used to see.

To Sam, KJ, and all of my dear, beloved PodSquad friends—as a certain angel of the Lord that we all love would say, "Knowing you has changed me." Getting back into podcasting with you all and being introduced to the wacky world of D&D has reminded me that joy, particularly queer joy, is foundational to survival and a life well lived.

To Maeve & Lilly—while one of you is an old friend and one of you is new, to say y'all occupy treasured places in my soul feels like an understatement. From helping me be myself as a kid when the world was trying to crush me, to being the one I leaned on when I needed to build myself back up in my early 30s, I could write a thousand books with a million words and not a single one of them would come close to conveying how much I adore you both.

To the therapists who got me through my five long months of intensive care in 2024, and the wonderful friends I made there, y'all know who you are. You all saw me at my categorical worst and still insisted there was light in me, and for that, you helped make me brighter than I could have ever been before.

To my parents and grandparents—though none of you lived long enough to read my works, know that you are in every letter I write, and in every word I pass down to the next generation.

To SEPTA—even when your buses run late or routes are weirdly detoured, you've always managed to carry me where I needed to be, and without the adventures I've had along your many routes over many years, this book simply would not exist.

To the city of Philadelphia, my beloved—from the Magic Gardens on South Street, to the hills of Germantown, from the heart of Kensington to Center City's LOVE Park, I am who I am because of your grit and your beauty. Know I go forth into every day of my time on this Earth with your tenacity and tenderness stitched into my every atom. Nowhere will ever feel more home than in the curves of your skyline and in the space between your rivers.

And as ever, to you reading this—don't rob the world of the chance to hear your story. Even as administrations rise and fall, you're still here through it all, and no one will ever be to this universe what you can. Live loud and love hard, and know that your verses matter now more than ever.

ABOUT THE AUTHOR

Elayna Mae Darcy is an author, podcast host, and chaotic good bard from Philadelphia (Go birds!). With a Film & Media Arts degree from Temple University, they have spent the last decade deeply involved in fandom communities, co-founding the local publisher, Elixir Verse Press, and releasing three books, UNRAVELING LIGHT (2018), DARKNESS UNDONE (2020), and the YA fantasy novel in verse, STILL THE STARS (2022). They have had pieces published in the *Wizards in Space*, *Impostor Lit*, *just femme & dandy*, and *Limited Editions*, and usually can be found in a local library or snuggling with their cat, Bean.

www.ingramcontent.com/pod-product-compliance
Lightning Source LLC
Chambersburg PA
CBHW060612080526
44585CB00013B/800